Strengthening Democracy in New York State

Thomas A. Chambers

PowerKiDS press.

New York

Published in 2015 by The Rosen Publishing Group, Inc.
29 East 21st Street, New York, NY 10010

Book Design: Chris Brand

Photo Credits: Cover, pp. 11 (both), 15, 19 Library of Congress Prints and Photographs Division, Washington, DC; cover (inset) Wikipedia/Mott Lucretia Painting Kyle 1841.jpg; cover (inset) Photo Researchers/Getty Images; p. 5 Wikipedia/Simeon DeWitt Central NY Military Tract.jpg; p. 7 Stock Montage/ Archive Photos/Getty Images; p. 9 fotog/Getty Images; p. 13 Heritage Images/ Hulton Archive/Getty Images; p. 17 (main) Buyenlarge/Archive Photos/Getty Images; p. 17 (inset) Universal History Archive/ Universal Image Group/Getty Images; p. 21 AP Images.

Library of Congress Cataloging-in-Publication Data

Chambers, Thomas A.
Strengthening Democracy in New York State / by Thomas A. Chambers.
p. cm. — (Spotlight on New York)
Includes index.
ISBN 978-1-4777-5180-0 (pbk.)
ISBN 978-1-4777-5183-1 (6-pack)
ISBN 978-1-4777-7277-5 (library binding)
1. New York (State)—Politics and government—Juvenile literature. 2. New York (N.Y.)—Juvenile literature. I. Chambers, Thomas A. II. Title.
JK3416.C49 2015
320.4747—d23

Manufactured in the United States of America

CPSIA Compliance Information: Batch #WS15RC: For further information contact Rosen Publishing, New York, New York at 1-800-237-9932.

Contents

New York After the Revolutionary War

After the **American Revolution**, New York State's government tried to put in place the ideals of **democracy** and equality many had fought for. White men who owned a certain amount of property could vote in elections. However, women, Native Americans, African Americans, and many poor whites weren't allowed to vote. Politics involved big rallies where men seeking election, many of them rich landowners, asked ordinary New Yorkers for their vote. This kind of campaigning and appealing to ordinary **citizens** was new, but farmers, workers, shopkeepers, and laborers wouldn't support politicians who didn't respect them.

As New York expanded west, many people got rich from buying and selling land. These **speculators** bought land from Revolutionary War soldiers who had been given acres in the state's western areas but couldn't afford to move there. Some settlers had already moved to this land and wanted to stay, but didn't have the required piece of paper showing they owned their property. This upset many New Yorkers, who thought it wasn't fair that speculators grew rich while poor soldiers and ordinary farmers lost out.

This map was made around 1792. It shows the lands set aside for New York soldiers who fought in the American Revolution.

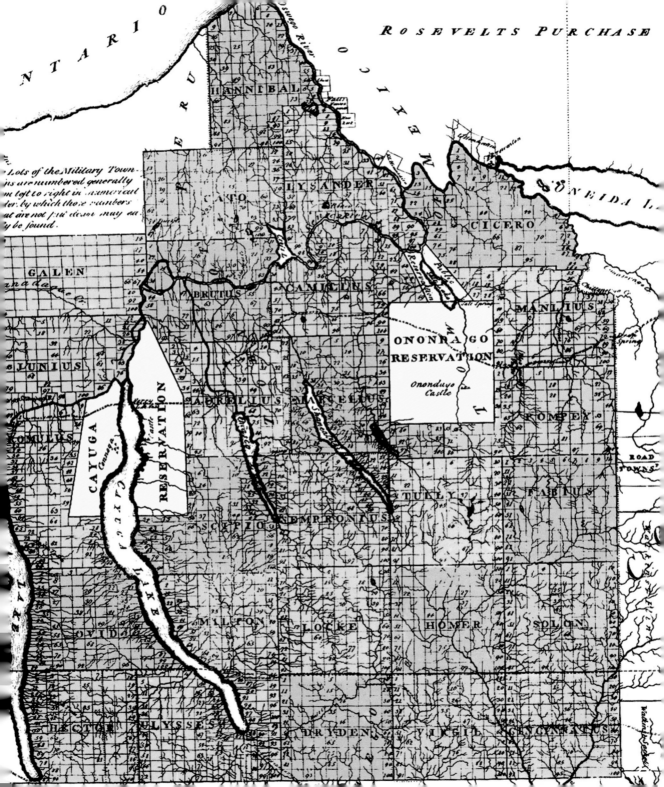

Native Americans in Early New York

Most of the land sold by New York State was taken from the tribes of the Iroquois Confederacy through **treaties**. Even the Oneida and some Tuscarora, who fought alongside the Patriots during the American Revolution, lost their land. **Missionaries** tried to convert the Iroquois tribes to Christianity and help them become like white settlers by living in frame houses, learning to read and write, not drinking alcohol, wearing clothing like white settlers, farming small plots of land, and owning property individually. This created divisions within the six Iroquois nations, with some groups who followed old Iroquois ways and some groups who became Christian.

By the middle of the 1800s, only a few thousand Iroquois still lived in New York State. The Seneca sold 2 million acres—all the land west of Seneca Lake—for only $5,000! Seven reservations were established, but they weren't large enough to support traditional Native American activities, including farming, hunting, and trapping. Many Iroquois remained in New York State, however, and began reviving their traditional culture under a movement led by Seneca **prophet** Handsome Lake.

This painting shows what life was like in an Iroquois village. The home in the center is called a longhouse. They were often large enough to provide shelter for several families.

Slavery in New York State

Slavery had existed in New York since the earliest Dutch period, and New York City served as a major base for slave-trading ships throughout the colonial era. Most enslaved Africans lived in New York City and on Hudson River valley **manors** owned by wealthy families. Many free blacks also made homes in the state and created strong communities and churches. Approximately 6,000 free blacks were eligible to vote in the 1820s. Some politicians felt African Americans weren't intelligent enough to vote and tried to disqualify free blacks. Others felt that if free blacks paid taxes, they should be allowed to vote if they paid an additional $250 fee, which was a lot of money back then!

In 1799, New York State decided slavery should end and passed a **gradual emancipation** law freeing all slaves born after July 4 of that year. What a great way to celebrate Independence Day! By 1827, groups like the New York **Manumission** Society succeeded in gaining freedom for all New York's slaves.

The Phillipsburg Manor house, shown here, was the center of activity for the 52,000-acre Phillipsburg Manor. The Philipses were one of the largest slave holders in the northern colonies. In 1750, 23 African slaves worked at Phillipsburg Manor.

The Abolitionist Movement

New Yorkers didn't stop with freeing their state's slaves—they wanted all people in the United States to be free. Among the leading **abolitionists** were Lewis Tappan and Gerrit Smith. However, many opposed their efforts. Rioters attacked Tappan's house in 1834 because they didn't want African Americans to gain equality. Attempts to change U.S. laws failed, and abolitionists decided to try to free individual slaves from the South, where slavery was still legal.

Churches across the state, and especially along the Erie Canal, opposed slavery because they thought it was against Christian teachings. They formed the basis of the abolitionist movement.

Many New Yorkers helped slaves escape to freedom along a series of routes called the Underground Railroad. The border with Canada, which didn't allow slavery, made New York a key part of this network. People like Harriet Tubman and Frederick Douglass, who had both escaped slavery, helped fellow African Americans reach freedom in Canada. Douglass and Samuel Cornish published newspapers spreading the abolitionist cause. They showed that African Americans were intelligent people and effective leaders.

Lewis Tappan

Gerrit Smith

Lewis Tappan and Gerrit Smith, shown here, were two of New York's most outspoken abolitionists. Taking a stand against slavery was dangerous even in the North, but both Tappan and Smith never stopped fighting for their beliefs.

New York and the Civil War

The **American Civil War** began in 1861. New York political parties were divided about the war. New York City mayor Fernando Wood even proposed leaving the United States! Rich men could avoid fighting by paying others to fight in their place. These **substitutes** were often poor Irish **immigrants**.

In 1863, riots broke out in Manhattan because new **draft** laws required men to fight in the war. Many white New Yorkers blamed free blacks for this. Nearly 120 people, mostly free blacks, died in the riots. Divisions over the war continued, but New York State contributed 360,000 soldiers, including several thousand free blacks, to the Union cause.

After the war, many **freedmen** looked for opportunities outside the South. By the 1890s, tens of thousands had migrated to growing industrial cities such as New York, Albany, Syracuse, Rochester, and Buffalo for factory jobs. Growing urban populations of African Americans created tensions with poor whites, many of whom were immigrants from Europe. Full equality and voting rights took many more years to achieve.

This is a depiction of a draft riot on New York City in 1863. The burning building is the Provost Marshall's Office, which was the headquarters for federal officials enforcing draft laws.

13

Women's Rights

Many of New York's key abolitionists were women. Leaders like Elizabeth Cady Stanton and Lucretia Mott argued that if slaves deserved freedom, women did, too. Women weren't full and equal citizens because they lacked many of the rights men had. Most women in New York State couldn't own property, none could vote, and using the courts or obtaining a divorce was very difficult. Women leaders in New York organized a **convention** at Seneca Falls in 1848 to demand full citizenship.

The convention issued a Declaration of Sentiments that looked a lot like the Declaration of Independence colonial leaders had issued at the beginning of the American Revolution. It listed everything men had done to **oppress** women. Many similar meetings took place in the years that followed, and New York State soon passed laws allowing women to control property they had owned before they were married or received during their marriage.

During Dutch colonial times, women had enjoyed some of these rights and even traded furs and goods. After the English took over in 1664, women lost some of their legal rights and engaged in less business. It took many years for women to gain equality.

Our Roll of Honor

Containing all the
Signatures to the "Declaration of Sentiments"
Set Forth by the First

Woman's Rights Convention,

held at
Seneca Falls, New York
July 19-20, 1848

LADIES:

Lucretia Mott
Harriet Cady Eaton
Margaret Pryor
Elizabeth Cady Stanton
Eunice Newton Foote
Mary Ann M'Clintock
Margaret Schooley
Martha C. Wright
Jane C. Hunt
Amy Post
Catherine F. Stebbins
Mary Ann Frink
Lydia Mount
Delia Mathews
Catherine C. Paine
Elizabeth W. M'Clintock
Malvina Seymour
Phebe Mosher
Catherine Shaw
Deborah Scott
Sarah Hallowell
Mary M'Clintock
Mary Gilbert

Sophronia Taylor
Cynthia Davis
Hannah Plant
Lucy Jones
Sarah Whitney
Mary H. Hallowell
Elizabeth Conklin
Sally Pitcher
Mary Conklin
Susan Quinn
Mary S. Mirror
Phebe King
Julia Ann Drake
Charlotte Woodward
Martha Underhill
Dorothy Mathews
Eunice Barker
Sarah R. Woods
Lydia Gild
Sarah Hoffman
Elizabeth Leslie
Martha Ridley

Rachel D. Bonnel
Betsey Tewksbury
Rhoda Palmer
Margaret Jenkins
Cynthia Fuller
Mary Martin
P. A. Culvert
Susan R. Doty
Rebecca Race
Sarah A. Mosher
Mary E. Vail
Lucy Spalding
Lovina Latham
Sarah Smith
Eliza Martin
Maria E. Wilbur
Elizabeth D. Smith
Caroline Barker
Ann Porter
Experience Gibbs
Antoinette E. Segur
Hannah J. Latham
Sarah Sisson

GENTLEMEN:

Richard P. Hunt
Samuel D. Tillman
Justin Williams
Elisha Foote
Frederick Douglass
Henry W. Seymour
Henry Seymour
David Spalding
William G. Barker
Elias J. Doty
John Jones

Willam S. Dell
James Mott
William Burroughs
Robert Smallbridge
Jacob Mathews
Charles L. Hoskins
Thomas M'Clintock
Saron Phillips
Jacob P. Chamberlain
Jonathan Metcalf

Nathan J. Milliken
S. E. Woodworth
Edward F. Underhill
George W. Pryor
Joel Bunker
Isaac VanTassel
Thomas Dell
E. W. Capron
Stephen Shear
Henry Hatley
Azaliah Schooley

This "Roll of Honor" lists the names of all who signed the Declaration of Sentiments at the 1848 Seneca Falls Woman's Rights Convention. Many women signed the declaration, but many men signed the document as well.

Women's Suffrage in New York State

Reformers also sought freedom for women in the way they dressed, and Amelia Bloomer said that instead of tight dresses, women should wear loose pants. People made fun of the "bloomers" she and other women wore, but the idea didn't die. Reformers at Oneida even went so far as to allow women to play baseball, something most people thought women were too weak to do! Today, many girls and women excel at sports, so Oneida had a good idea.

Seneca Falls didn't achieve its main aim of gaining the vote for women, but women like Susan B. Anthony became major leaders of the **suffrage** movement. They marched and protested for equal rights, with many wives and daughters of wealthy New Yorkers demanding the vote. In 1917, New York State granted women the vote, becoming one of the first states to do so. The United States granted all women citizens suffrage with the 19th **Amendment** to the Constitution, passed in 1920. New York led the nation in working for equality once again.

Susan B. Anthony is one of the most famous suffragettes in history. Suffragettes are women who fought for voting rights, such as the women in the photograph shown here.

DENMARK
ON THE VERGE OF WAR
GAVE WOMEN THE VOTE
WHY NOT GIVE IT TO
AMERICAN WOMEN NOW

Susan B. Anthony

Migration

From the state's earliest days, New Yorkers came from all over the world. People fleeing ethnic and religious **persecution** formed a key part of the Dutch colony. The forced migration of Africans as slaves to the Dutch and English colonies increased New York's population, too.

One of the biggest changes in New York State during the late 1800s was the arrival of many immigrants from southern and eastern Europe. Italian, Jewish, Russian, Polish, Greek, and various Slavic people, to name just a few of the nationalities, moved into neighborhoods where their countrymen also lived. They spoke foreign languages, worshipped differently, and ate unusual foods, at least in the minds of New Yorkers who had lived there for many years or who came from places such as England.

By 1900, half of New Yorkers lived in a big city, and one-fourth had been born in another country. Cities like New York became very crowded with the hundreds of thousands of new arrivals, including many African Americans who left the South, and living and working conditions were terrible. Families squeezed into tiny apartments called **tenements**, which had few windows and no indoor plumbing.

Many immigrants settled in New York City because the ships that brought them to the United States from their home countries docked at Ellis Island. New York City was the closest major city to this immigration station.

19

Improved Working Conditions

Immigrants worked whatever jobs they could find. They often took dirty and low-paying work, as in slaughterhouses (where animals were killed for food), tanneries (where chemicals turned animal hides into leather), or textile mills (where clothes were made). Sometimes young children worked alongside their parents in dangerous conditions. Many people were injured or died in these factories. Some workers even had to pay the factory owners for the electricity that ran the machines they worked on!

To improve their working conditions and to earn more money, many immigrant workers formed **labor unions**. A strike in 1909 by almost 30,000 women in the textile mills won better pay and shorter hours for most textile workers, but didn't end all the harsh conditions. In 1911, about 146 women died in a fire at New York City's Triangle Shirtwaist Factory. It took many more years for unions to fully help women and for New York State to pass laws protecting workers and forbidding child labor.

This photograph shows firefighters trying to put out the deadly blaze at the Triangle Shirtwaist Factory. It was a common practice to lock the doors to a factory's exits to keep workers from taking unnecessary breaks. This trapped the workers inside after the fire broke out.

Equality for All

New Yorkers have been trying to figure out what "democracy" and "citizenship" mean since the earliest days of European settlement. The American Revolution set high ideals for equality and opportunity. When New Yorkers felt their nation's ideals weren't being met, they demanded change. Organizations such as abolitionist societies, women suffrage associations, and labor unions fought for equal rights and more opportunity for all. The Iroquois gave women a strong role in governing their communities, probably the first attempts at equal rights in the land that became New York State. Iroquois concepts of respecting individual groups and reaching decisions by **consensus** also showed how people could get along together.

It wasn't always possible to achieve these goals because not everyone shared them or understood them in the same way. Sometimes different nationalities fought each other for jobs or power. Speculators cheated the Iroquois and poor settlers out of their land. But New Yorkers kept working to make their state better and to help achieve the promise of equality stated in the Declaration of Independence: "that all men are created equal" and have the right to "life, liberty and the pursuit of happiness."

Glossary

abolitionists: People who fight to end slavery.

amendment: A change or an addition to a constitution.

American Civil War: A war fought from 1861 to 1865 in the United States between the Union (the Northern states) and the Confederacy (the Southern states).

American Revolution: The war that the American colonists fought from 1775 to 1783 to win independence from England.

citizens: Residents of a place who have certain rights.

consensus: A general agreement about something.

convention: A large meeting or conference, especially of members of a political party or a particular profession.

democracy: A form of government in which citizens vote to elect leaders.

draft: Having to do with a system in which young men are required to join the military for a period of time.

freedmen: Slaves who became free after the American Civil War.

gradual emancipation: A process for moving away from slavery by granting freedom to people who were born to slaves after a given date, or when slaves reached a certain age.

immigrants: People who move to another country, usually for permanent residence.

labor unions: Organized associations of workers formed to protect and further their rights and interests.

manors: Large tracts of land in colonial New York occupied by people who paid the landowner or crown money to live there.

manumission: The act of releasing someone from slavery.

missionaries: People who are sent to a foreign country to do religious work.

oppress: To treat a person or group in a cruel or unfair way.

persecution: The act of being cruel to someone because of their race, gender, religion, or political beliefs.

prophet: A member of a religion who delivers messages that are believed to have come from a god.

speculators: People who invest money in ways that could produce a large profit but that also involve a lot of risk.

substitutes: People who stand in for others.

suffrage: The right to vote.

tenements: Rooms or sets of rooms inside a home where people live.

treaties: Official agreements between countries or groups.

Index

Primary Source List

Cover. *Inez Hilholland.* Created by Bain News Service. Negative. 1913. Now kept at the Library of Congress Prints and Photographs Division, Washington, DC.

Cover (inset). *Fredrick Douglass.* Oil on canvas. ca. 1844. Now kept at the National Portrait Gallery, Washington, DC.

Cover (inset). *Painting of Lucretia Mott.* Created by Joseph Kyle. Oil on canvas. 1842. Now kept at the National Portrait Gallery, Washington, DC.

Page 5. *Central New York State (1793).* Created by Simeon De Witt. Drawing. 1793. Now kept at the American Geographical Society Library at the University of Wisconsin-Milwaukee, Milwaukee, WI.

Page 11. *Hon. Gerrit Smith of N.Y.* Photographic print. Between 1855 and 1865. Now kept at the Library of Congress Prints and Photographic Print, Washington, DC.

Page 11 (inset). *The Late Lewis Tappan.* Wood engraving. 1873. Now kept at the Library of Congress Prints and Photographs Division, Washington, DC.

Page 15. *Declaration of Sentiments.* Pamphlet. 1848. Now kept at the Library of Congress Miller NAWSA Scrapbook Collections, Washington, DC.

Page 17. *New York Pickets at the White House.* Photographic Print. 1917. Now kept at the Library of Congress Prints and Photographs Division, Washington, DC.

Page 17 (inset). *Susan B. (Susan Brownell) Anthony, 1820 – 1906.* Created by Frances Benjamin Johnston. Photographic print. ca. 1890 – 1910. Now kept at the Library of Congress Prints and Photographs Division, Washington, DC.

Page 19. *Mulberry Street, New York City.* Created by Detroit Publishing Co. Photographic print. ca. 1900. Now kept at the Library of Congress Prints and Photographs Division, Washington, DC.

Page 21. *Triangle Fire.* Created by Brown Brothers. Photographic print. 1911. Now kept at the Kheel Center at Cornell University, Ithaca, NY.

Websites

Due to the changing nature of Internet links, Rosen Publishing has developed an online list of websites related to the subject of this book. This site is updated regularly. Please use this link to access the list: http://www.rcbmlinks.com/nysh/stny